THE VIKING INVADER — WE TELL IT LIKE IT IS

WHY DO WE DO IT?

Leading Viking Captain Rolf Rottgutt Reveals All...

Shipmates...

People often come up to me and say, "Hey, Captain Rottgutt, what gives with the raiding and terror? Why don't you stay home and farm like everybody else?"

So I tell them:
• Fighting's fun, and if you're killed you go to Valhalla.
• Raiding is a profitable way of spending the summer.
• You can do all the farming you want in spring and autumn.
• If you want to make a name for yourself in politics, start by being a successful raider.
• And the look of surprise on people's faces when they see us coming is worth all

Here's a map for our readers, so they'll know where all the places we talk about actually are.

the gold in Gotland.

Then people usually say, "Why are they surprised? Don't they spend their time fighting off invaders? What makes you so different?"

So I tell them...
• What makes us surprising is that we're so unexpected. People are used to being attacked by land, and usually get wind of it in advance. Us? We've got long-ships and can strike out of the blue. Before they've got time to say "Isn't that somebody coming to raid us? Put my porridge in the warm oven," we're all over them.
• And we go in and out of Europe's rivers like a dose of salts.

Then people ask how much I earn doing this, and I say:
• That's for me to know and you to find out. But I didn't get to live in a large house with several wives and lots of slaves just by being a farmer. Geddit?

Best wishes

Rolf Rottgutt

The Viking Invader

was written by
FERGUS FLEMING

and designed by
KAREN TOMLINS

Editor
PAUL DOWSWELL

Historical consultant
DR JOHN HAYWOOD

Illustrations by Guy Smith, Rodney Matthews and Gerald Wood.

VIKING INVADER ON OTHER PAGES

KING ALF
SPLITS UP ENGLAND

King Alf. A very good king, but (allegedly) no good at baking cakes.

886

"You're there – we're here," says Wessex man

Vikings are reeling after a stunning setback in England. King Alfred the Great of Wessex, who was defeated by the Great Heathen Horde eight years ago, has returned with a vengeance!

In a miraculous comeback Anglo-Saxon Alf scored a series of knockout victories which drove the invaders out of Wessex. He even forced his opposite number, Danish king Guthrum, and 30 of his top officers, to become Christians. Now he's finalized the business by making them sign a treaty saying who owns what.

Foot

"Basically, we were caught on the wrong foot," said Guthrum. "All our best men had settled down on the farmland they conquered, and there weren't enough of us left to raise an army to fight the enemy."

Under the new arrangement the Vikings have to stay in an area called the Danelaw, which runs up the east side of England. Everything else belongs to the Anglo-Saxon locals.

Cross

"Well, it could be worse," said Guthrum. "It's good farming country and I'm sure a lot of Anglo-Saxons will be crossing the border to live here. The advantages are endless. Here in the Danelaw – we invented the word "law" by the way – we've got a fantastic legal system, with local courts and a jury. They don't have anything like that in Wessex."

"What's more, we have the nearest thing to democracy this country will have for centuries. If you have 25 acres and a couple of cows, you can come to one of our assemblies and join in with the decision-making.

It's not quite what you might call a parliament or senate. I don't know what they call them in Wessex, but back home we just call them *Things*."

BYZANTIUM THROWS IN THE TOWEL

907

FREE BATHS FOR ALL

Russian Vikings were in a real lather yesterday as they celebrated a major victory over Byzantium.

Representatives of Viking King Oleg of Kiev sailed over the Black Sea to Constantinople, capital of the Byzantine Empire. They walked around the city walls, and told the Emperor that unless he came up with a deal pretty quickly they'd sack the place.

They left with numerous trading privileges, open access to the city and the promise of as many free baths as they liked.

"Appearances are very important in this part of the world," explained Admiral Ingjald. "If you go into battle looking rumpled and grubby the enemy simply won't have anything to do with you."

Vikings setting up camp outside Constantinople.

STOP PRESS
GRAFFITI ANGER

Offended Byzantine citizens have lodged a complaint about a piece of Viking graffiti. The offending runes, carved into a marble balustrade in their cathedral Hagia Sophia, read "Halfdan was here".

Church authorities have launched an immediate investigation to find the culprit.

"Who are you calling smug?" says Rollo of Normandy. "I just happen to be an extremely clever Viking!"

CRAFTY KING IN SHOW OF NORMAN WISDOM

ROLLO TO RULE AT ROUEN

911

King Charles the Simple of France, great-great-grandson of Charlemagne, has pulled off a masterstroke. He's persuaded one bunch of Vikings to protect him from the others!

"I was getting fed up," said Charles. "Every year the Vikings would sail up the River Seine to attack Paris, and every year I had to pay them to go away. So I went up to this Danish fellow, Rollo, and said to him, 'Hey Rollo! How'd you like to rule Normandy? It's lovely. Got a fantastic capital at Rouen. And it's really well placed on the mouth of the River Seine. It's all yours. All you have to do in return is become a Christian and promise to stop any Vikings coming up the river. If you're good, every ten years or so I'll give you some more land. How about it?' Well, he almost bit my hand off, he was that eager."

Smorgasbord

Vikings are astonished at the betrayal. "He's a two-timing, no-good, son-of-a-smorgasbord!" fumed a Norwegian raider. "What a turncoat!"

But Rollo isn't taking any notice. He's got big ambitions for Normandy. At Rouen yesterday he unveiled his plan to make the Normans the most feared people in Europe.

"We'll out-Vike the Vikings!" he boasted. "We'll invade Italy and Sicily and best of all, we'll conquer England in 1066. And because I'm a man of my word, we won't invade France – not much, at any rate – and we'll keep Paris safe from invasion."

"Don't listen to what they're saying in Scandinavia. I'm a sweetie really."

DANELAW DOWN THE DRAIN

954

BLOODAXE AXED

King Eric Bloodaxe of York is down in the dumps today. And not just because he's dead! Eric has just lost the last piece of Viking territory in England.

Eric, ex-king of Norway and now ex-king of York, did his best during a brief, six-year reign to restore Viking control over England.

"He had an uphill struggle," confessed an anonymous source. "He had to fight off the Anglo-Saxons, who were gradually conquering the Danelaw. He had to defend himself against the Scots, who are a tough bunch at the best of times. On top of that he had to deal with King Olaf Sihtricson of Dublin who decided he wanted a bit of the action too."

End

The end came when Eric was driven out of York by an army of Northumbrians and killed in an ambush. This left the way open for Anglo-Saxon King Eadred to march in and declare himself King of all England.

"Alas, poor Eric!" said Eadred. "He suffered the slings and arrows of outrageous fortune. Unlike me."

With Eric's tragic death his followers have thrown aside their swords and picked up their trowels. "We're through with all that Viking stuff," said a leading Yorkshireman. "No more raids and fearsome facial hair in the wee hours. From now on we're going to concentrate on allotment gardening."

But old habits die hard. Only last week three young men were found headless in an alleyway. Locals say they had scoffed at an ailing stand of runner beans.

Eric (far right), and his Viking pals pack their bags at York. Ambush ahoy!

15. The only promise a Viking was allowed to break was:
a) a peace treaty with a foreigner
b) that he'd do the washing up
c) that he'd be home before midnight
d) one made on a Friday

16. In Denmark, if you wanted to be a pirate you had to have:
a) a permit
b) a reputation
c) a big beard
d) a parrot and an eye patch

17. Vikings hunted elk on:
a) foot
b) skis
c) Wednesdays
d) horseback

18. Vikings made skates out of:
a) pieces of wood
b) horses' hooves
c) old swords
d) whale ribs.

19. In 850 the Anglo-Saxons defeated a Viking fleet at:
a) Snak
b) Sandwich
c) Hamburger
d) Hottdhogg

20. The man who saved Paris from the Vikings in 885 was called:
a) Odo
b) Odon't
c) Hedid
d) Henever

CHECK YOUR ANSWERS ON THE RIGHT OF THIS PAGE...

MAIDENS ONLY

MARRIAGE

WHAT EVERY VIKING MAIDEN SHOULD KNOW

By the Invader's matrimony correspondent Great Aunt Freydis

Those of you who have not had the opportunity to travel, will be unaware that Viking women have a great deal more independence and respect than women in other parts of the world. But like everywhere else, we still get married here. Before you lies a life of domestic bliss. So what CAN you expect? Read on, dear girls, and I will REVEAL ALL!

Finding Mr. Right

Your parents will usually choose your husband. You will probably marry for financial or political reasons, rather than love. (This is especially likely if you come from a wealthy and important family.)

Ker-ching

Before you marry, your husband-to-be gives your father a gift of goods and property in exchange for you. Then your father gives him goods and money for taking you off his hands. If this makes YOU feel like a bit of property yourself, don't worry – when you marry, all of these goods will actually belong to YOU!

An embroidery, yesterday. This is what you'll spend a great deal of time doing once you're wed.

Buuuurpp

Your marriage is celebrated with a huge feast. This sounds quite fun, but expect to see ghastly Uncle Harald from Uppsala, and dreary Aunt Asa from Trelleborg. The bad news is – if you're really rich the party could go on for a WHOLE MONTH.

The torture never stops

Unless you're rich enough to have slaves your wifely duties will include: cooking, baking, brewing beer, making all the clothes your family needs, weaving blankets and tapestries, and (of course) looking after the children.

Oh no, there's more

Not only that, if hubby is a farmer then you'll have to milk the cows and feed the chickens. And you'll have to sort out all the household finances. AND you'll have to nurse any sick members of the family. AND you'll have to run the family business if hubby's off trading or raiding.

Grate escape

So what happens if twinkle-eyed Sven with the merry laugh and winning smile turns into a sour old goat who never changes his tunic. Simple. You announce you wish to be divorced in front of a group of witnesses and you're an older and wiser FREE WOMAN. Not only that, you get to keep the goods and property you brought to the marriage in the first place. NOT BAD EH? (Mind you, sour old Sven can divorce you just as easily, so go easy on the nagging!)

NEXT WEEK: FRESH WAYS WITH HERRING

THE AXE FILES THE ANSWERS!

1. c) Viking means "plunderer". 2. a) The Swedes by a long way. Rune-stone tally: Sweden 2,500, Denmark 180, Norway 45. 3. a) They wore flares – and they probably wore gold medallions too. 4. c) Trick question! Vikings weren't animal rights sympathizers. But they did wear fake furs made out of cloth. 5. a) His full name was Eystein Fart. 6. c) Because they hadn't discovered sugar the Vikings had better teeth than most people today. 7. c) His wife gave him a special pair of non-flammable breeches in case he had to fight a dragon. They were made from extra-thick fur boiled in pitch and rolled in sand. But, by the way, some Vikings did wear enormous, bristly knickerbockers. 8. b) Charles the Fat. 9. a) Streets were paved with wood. 10. a) Willow twigs kept them snug. 11. a) The poem was in praise of Erik Blood-Axe, who was about to have Egil executed. Erik was so impressed that he gave Egil a pardon. 12. b) Apart from being an important city York had a thriving comb industry. They made the combs out of antlers. 13. c) He died celebrating the death of an enemy. 14. b) Vikings suffered from carbon monoxide poisoning. When it was too cold to venture outside, their houses filled with smoke because they didn't have chimneys. 15. a) A Viking was expected to keep his word at all times unless it was a peace treaty made abroad. 16. a) In the eleventh century the King of Denmark made a lot of money licensing would-be pirates. 17. b) They hunted them on skis, using bows and arrows. 18. b) They used horses' foot bones. 19. b) Sandwich, of course. 20. a) Count Odo kept the Vikings out of Paris in 885 and drove them out of France four years later.

ODIN AND FRIGG

It's warrior Odin, the father of all other gods, with his two nosy ravens, who tell him what's going on in the world. His wife Frigg, the mother goddess, is by his side. She loves humans and can see into the future. One look at this sail tells your enemies they don't *have* a future!

THOR

The god of law, order and thunder who wields a mighty hammer. Thor rides on his chariot with two goats, Toothgnasher and Toothgrinder. He's friendly but dim, and there's nothing he likes better than an almighty scrap. He's the perfect role model, and an inspiration to your crew!

LOKI

He's Odin's brother and god of trickery. Handsome and clever, he can change shape to become any animal he chooses. But he's seriously evil too – and out to stir up all kinds of mischief. Just the fellow to put you in the mood for a good pillage.

FREYA

The goddess of love and beauty will keep you company on those long, lonely voyages. But, as you know, she's also the goddess of death. What more could an axe-wielding, blood-lusting looter ask for...

FENRIR

Offspring of Loki and Angrboda (a giantess). Fenrir is a wolf who's chained to a rock. When he breaks free he'll bring about Ragnarok – the end of the world*. Gives your foes a clear message – it's certainly the end of the world for them!

YMIR

Strictly speaking, Ymir is a frost giant, rather than a god. As we all know, Odin killed him and made the world out of chunks of his body. Ymir is guaranteed to make your enemy's blood turn to ice in an instant.

*Myth fans! Ragnarok will be marked by very cold weather, the Earth sinking into the sea and all life vanishing. Only two humans will survive. (Just hope it isn't you and that ghastly bloke from Småland you met last spring when you were pillaging Northumbria.)